*For those in Southern Appalachia who endured the
destruction of Hurricane Helene on September 27th, 2024
and in the mournful months that followed.*

For all who walk the path of loss and suffering.

After the Storm
(Poems and Prayers)

petermivey.substack.com
fourseasonssoulcare.org

ISBN: 979-8-9882822-8-0

FIRST PRINT EDITION NOVEMBER 2025

Copper Finch Publishing
Newton, NC 28658
(712) 310-7426
https://copperfinchpublishing.com

After the Storm is a work of heartfelt grace—a collection of words and images that express the pain and resilience of those who have experienced loss. Through its evocative language and haunting beauty, it invites us to see God's faithfulness even in the broken branches and flooded valleys of our lives. Both a lament and a hymn of resurrection, this collection gently reminds us that even amid life's fiercest winds, healing and new beginnings quietly emerge from the ruins. Each page lovingly directs us toward God's steadfast love, which tenderly transforms devastation into the quiet hope of renewal.

Fil Anderson, author of *Running on Empty*

Peter's poems are portals to look back and to look within, to look alone, and also to look together. To remember what happened and what happened inside of us as we lived through Helene's fury. In those terrible winds, we experienced a terror like no other. But in our recovery, we see a love that is possible and an invitation to continue. Peter's poems are our invitation to not just recover but to live well as we recover from tragedies that we thought would be our end. *After the Storm* is a beautiful and important book of remembering the brutal and beautiful to come.

Stephen W. Smith, author of *The Lazarus Life* and *Greening: Poems in the Unfolding of Our Lives*

This book is for anyone who has endured a shattering, whether through a storm like Hurricane Helene or any other gut-wrenching, life-altering grief. In his intimate poetry, Peter reveals his raw emotions and innermost thoughts from inside the storm—a struggle he and so many others are just beginning to process. A gift and a companion, this collection offers solace to anyone who needs healing.

Kaylene Derkson, President of The Soul Care Institute

In *After the Storm*, Peter Ivey writes from a real and rooted place—his words rising from the soil of Southern Appalachia and the lived grief of a community forever changed. In these poems, the universal ache of loss meets the particularity of place and person, reminding us that incarnation always happens somewhere. Ivey gives voice to what it means to grieve, pray, endure, and hope amid the upheaval of natural disaster. Ivey's attentive eye and contemplative heart remind us that beauty and belonging can still be found in the wreckage, and that healing begins with presence and Presence. At a time of climate insecurity and collective dislocation, Ivey does not look away from the devastation, but attends to it tenderly, helping us glimpse how beauty and belonging can emerge, even here, after the storm.

Tara M. Owens, CSD, CSDS, Executive Director of Anam Cara Ministries and author of Embracing the Body: Finding God In Our Flesh & Bone

After the Storm

(poems and prayers)

Peter M. Ivey

Contents

We remember the night. We remember the angry, unrepentant clouds. We remember the wind like waves. We remember the rain, the rain, the rivers. We remember the trees falling, breaking, bending. We remember the curtain of dawn cruelly drawn, the presentation of isolation, lost communication. We remember our neighbors, the unsolicited favors, the gathering in driveways to catch our only news on car radios. We remember the body counts, rising, the missing, rising. We remember the train of helicopters, planes, vans, and trucks full of strangers offering help from every state. We remember the prayers and best wishes, the out-of-touch donations. We remember the taste of plastic water, the sound of lost power, the towering surge of sorrow as we stood in a place swept away. We remember the layers of loss like bedsheets. We remember the day, and the next, and the next.

Peter M. Ivey
August 2, 2025
West Jefferson, NC

just breathe

lord,
    have mercy

            christ,
                have mercy

                    lord,
                        have mercy

                                christ,
                                    have mercy

                                            lord,
                                        have mercy

                                christ,
                            have mercy

                    lord,
                have mercy

            christ,
    have mercy

lord,
    have mercy

            christ,
                have mercy

                    lord,
                        have mercy

                                christ,
                                    have mercy

1

i am coming undone...

o god,

would you please lean down

                and meet me with your soft mother-eyes

and throw your hidden trunk around me like an elephant in the Namib

                       at the body of her crumpled calf

and lift me

                  above these dark clouds so that i can see

something other than the swelling rain...

A Kind Word for Yourself

There is no need to know
all that you need
right now.

As the dark mud slowly dries,
and the streets receive a mournful dust,
allow yourself the grace

to rise and fall
like the unapologetic
floodwaters.

At 9am, you may be a dam about to breach,
at 3pm a rambling stream,
a bone-dry creek.

Others will say
slow down, step up,
reach in, cry out,

and, God bless 'em,
that may be just what they need.

Your own needs will come to light
as surely as the land will heal.

So when contractions come,
and your soul gives way,

let yourself be held,
and know.

When you are overwhelmed by the immensity of it all, remember this—

God is big enough;
  you are seen.

God is big enough;
  you are heard.

God is big enough;
  you are known.

God is big enough;
  you are loved.

Dry Bones

after Ezekiel

We now find ourselves lying
  In the middle of the valley of dry bones,
  Flayed open by the river's sword…

We look to the left,
  And our homes have washed away.
We turn to the right,
  And our neighbors have been swallowed by the earth.
We reach for each other,
  Dizzy with loss and disbelief…

We now find ourselves lying
  In the middle of the valley of dry bones,
  And we cry out to You for mercy.

Will these dry bones live?
  Will these dry bones live?
O Lord, you know. *You know!*
  So cause Your breath to blow.

Bring these bones to rattling,
  Lay sinew, muscle, and skin.
Set our feet to dancing,
  Bring the valley to life again.

When a Long Road Lies Ahead

Time must be taken,
A steady rhythm found,

One step, then the next,
Toes pressed into the ground.

Breathe in, then breathe out,
Trust the beat in your chest,

Mind that you're human—
Choose beauty, stillness, rest.

Name your companions,
Let your heart break with friends,

Yield to the Spirit,
Let your searching soul bend.

Sight the horizon,
Hold your face toward the stars,

Their light will guide you,
Illuminate the dark,

Until one day you wake,
Softly, suddenly undone,

by a sacred silence, singing,
Home is already won.

Sabbath

Rest is an arduous task
at a time like this…

The questions turn
unceasingly—

When do we return?
 How long must we wait?
Are we doing enough?
 Do we have what it takes?

My inner compass spins,
my mind overheats, I leave the ground,

 I am lost,
 I am found

by a quiet fog, the crickets' call,
and an effervescent cardinal singing .
her native song.

Slowly, slowly, cautiously, bare,
I let myself fall like chaff into a warm bath
of earth and God and skin.

When you wake up with a case of the morning 'shoulds'

Comparison is the thief
of the life you are meant to live
today

(& scrolling is not the remedy).

Some have the gift of time,
others expertise, & many
a drive to prove
their worth
through
an ever -
endless
- do -
gooding.

So close your eyes,
listen closely for the silence who
set your one-off magic into motion,

& breathe out
the delicious verity
that is you.

Sibling Rivalry

Tah-kee-os-tee is calm today,
lying back into her ancient groove,
showing off her latest and greatest collection
of storm-bought goods.

She drifts along in silence
as the sun glints off debris
high in the trees.

I can't bring myself to look at her.

Yesterday, you were our lifeblood,
our sister and friend! But today,
I know you by a new name—

Po-ko-kyu-ran-te.

How can you move on
while we still muck out your mud?
Don't you see what you've done?

She offers no reply, only presence
And her confident gaze downstream..

Back home, I watch the bees
Roll through the garden.

I hear my sister's whisper.

*Tah-kee-os-tee: a Cherokee name for the French Broad River
**Po-ko-kyu-ran-te: the pronunciation of the Italian word
"pococurante," meaning "caring little" or "indifferent

After-tension

I.

The trees call out like a pod of orca,
and I am filled with felicity and fright,
not knowing which way they might break,
toward the darkness, or toward the light.

II.

Even the creeks and the trees
now feel untamed (as if they ever weren't),
but oh how much beauty
they still hold!

here/now

backyard / wet grass /

my breath / striking the match /

alone at last / one month, how, how? /

ravens weaving, balking / cars turbulent like wind /

Cooper rolling, barking / autumn pinching my fingertips /

grey clouds smothering pale blue skies / black shadows cast

on the white chair / heat radiating from fire and loss /

low-light glowing lime-green through fading

leaves / my heart kicking, my body

being held / a rush to escape,

a sure whisper to

remain

First Rain

A month to the day,

the mountain rains return

with their haunting winds

and churning clouds of purple hue,

but this time,

everything is different.

Everything Feels Like Trying

Everything feels like trying
to roll a boulder—

parenthood,
and the laundry, of course,
but also the neighborhood walk,
a warm shower,

       stillness,

and it frightens me...

I kneel down in the living room
near the velvet-green couch, eyes closed,
heart clinched tighter than the lid on a pickle jar.

I push Cooper away until he breaks the seal
with his kind eyes and a reaching paw, saying

All I want is to be with you...

A Liturgy for Your Body on a Sunday Morning

As your thoughts saunter their way back
from the fading song of night,
allow them to linger like a wistful cloud
in a windless sky.

With your eyelids still drawn,
stretch out your limbs with the gentle force
of, say, a cicada breaking ground, or the nudge
of a breeze behind a dandelion seed.

Feel the softness of the sheets
against your God-knit skin.
Fill the mountain of your chest
with the air of the hour,
holding it like a pearl.

When you are ready,
(and only when you are ready),
open your eyes, and welcome the return of light.

Lie here as long as you would like.

When the moment to grace
your world makes itself known,
lay your grave linens aside with thanksgiving,
kiss both feet to the floor, and rise.

Blue Ridge Forest

No, those that survive are still in mourning,
　I can feel it in my limbs.
They stand more silent than before,
　keeping vigil for their fallen friends.
The horror it must have been, the bending,
　the earth giving way under foot,
first light…

We will never be the same,
　not the poplar, the spruce, the pine,
nor those of us who find our solace in these woods.
　The memory holds from root to crown,
I touch the trees, the forest grieves
　with hands held high.

Even Slower

Put down whatever you are doing.

Stuff every would, could, and should

back into the lovely reaches of your inner drawer,

and remember this:

you are only six weeks removed from the moment

you were told goodbye by what-was.

So move slowly.

No, beloved…

even slower.

About the Author

Peter M. Ivey is a spiritual director, contemplative retreat facilitator, and the founder of Four Seasons Soul Care. He is a graduate of Denver Seminary (MA Leadership), Furman University (BA Religion), and the Soul Care Institute. Peter is also the co-author of *Solo: Creating Space with God*. He and his wife, Becca, live in Asheville, NC with their three children and their dog, Cooper. You can connect with Peter at *www.fourseasonssoulcare.org* or *petermivey.substack.com*.

Acknowledgements

In many ways, I wish this collection didn't exist...It took a horrific storm to get here, and it isn't an experience I would like to live again. In the days and weeks that followed Helene, I turned to the reading and writing of poetry to help me process, pray, and grieve. Poetry was nearly the only means through which I could communicate what I was feeling. It was a lifeline, a balm, a saving grace in the midst of confusion and loss.

I've been sitting with these poems for over a year now, and if it wasn't for a number of wonderful people, you wouldn't be holding this beautiful book in your hands today. I'd like to take a moment to thank a few of them.

To Luke Hankins, thank you for your willingness to work with such a green poet. I am so grateful for your editing expertise, your gentle guidance, and honest feedback. You helped each of these poems to breath more deeply. Thank you.

To Tyler King at Copper Finch Publishing, thank you for being willing to take a risk on me. Your reaction to this collection was such a gift, one that spurs me on to keep picking up the pen. I am grateful for your partnership.

To my friend and mentor, Stephen W. Smith, if it wasn't for you, not only would I not be reading or writing poetry, but I wouldn't know the poet that's been living within me all along. Thank you for always reminding me of the truth—that we are all the beloved of God.

To my best friend, my bride, Becca, thank you for always cheering me on in my wild pursuits. I love you. And to our three soul-bendingly beautiful children, I pray that in your own moments of sorrow and grief (all of which I wish I could save you from), you would discover the infinitude of God's buoying love.

Finally, to you, the reader, thank you for being here, and for being who you are. I'd like to leave you with an Irish blessing.

May the road rise to meet you, May the wind always be at your back, May the sun shine warm upon your face, and rains fall soft upon your fields. And until we meet again, may God hold you in the palm of His hand.